Making a Budget

Cavendish
Square
New York

Carolyn E. W. Spath

Published in 2015 by Cavendish Square Publishing, LLC
243 5th Avenue, Suite 136, New York, NY 10016

Website: cavendishsq.com

This publication represents the opinions and views of the author based on his or her personal experience, knowledge, and research. The information in this book serves as a general guide only. The author and publisher have used their best efforts in preparing this book and disclaim liability rising directly or indirectly from the use and application of this book.

CPSIA Compliance Information: Batch #WW15CSQ

All websites were available and accurate when this book was sent to press.

Library of Congress Cataloging-in-Publication Data

Spath, Carolyn E.W.
Making a budget / Carolyn E.W. Spath.
pages cm. — (First-glance finance)
Includes index.
ISBN 978-1-50260-099-8 (hardcover) ISBN 978-1-50260-100-1 (ebook)
1. Finance, Personal—Juvenile literature. 2. Budgets, Personal—Juvenile literature. 3. Financial literacy—Juvenile literature. 4. Finance—Juvenile literature. I. Title.

HG179.S55285 2015
332.024—dc23

2014025525

Editor: Amy Hayes
Senior Copy Editor: Wendy A. Reynolds
Art Director: Jeffrey Talbot
Senior Designer: Amy Greenan
Senior Production Manager: Jennifer Ryder-Talbot
Production Editor: David McNamara
Photo Research by J8 Media

Printed in the United States of America

CONTENTS

CHAPTER ONE

Introducing Budgets

I f you had $10.00 right now, do you know what you would do with it? Would you spend it all on a new toy, or use it to buy several different things? Deciding on the best way to spend your money can be hard, but planning ahead of time can help you spend money wisely. The best way to do this is by making a **budget.**

What Is a Budget?

A budget is a plan for how money will be used. Budgets are based on **income** and **expenses**. Income is money

Planning how to spend your allowance is a simple form of budgeting.

you receive or earn, and expenses are the things you spend your money on.

When budgeting, you may need to look at your **expected income** and expenses, which is the money you plan to receive or spend in the future. Think about that imaginary $10.00 again. If I were to say, "I will give you $10.00 on Friday," that $10.00 would be your expected income. On Friday, when you receive the $10.00, it is just income. The things you would spend your $10.00 of income on, such as toys, snacks, or a movie ticket, would be expenses. Making a budget for the $10.00 is a way to decide what you want to spend the money on and **allocate** a certain portion of your income for each expense. When you allocate money, you set it aside for a specific use.

In a balanced budget, your expenses cannot be greater than your income. If you only have $10.00, you could plan to spend $2.00 on candy and $8.00 on a movie ticket. You could not budget $8.00 for a movie ticket and $4.00 for popcorn because you would not have enough money.

Balanced Budget

Income	Expenses
	$2.00 Candy
$10.00 Gift	+ $8.00 Movie Ticket

Total Income	**Total Expenses**
$10.00 **=**	$10.00

Unbalanced Budget

Income	Expenses
	$4.00 Popcorn
$10.00 Gift	+ $8.00 Movie Ticket

Total Income	**Total Expenses**
$10.00 **≠**	$12.00

These charts show the difference between a balanced and an unbalanced budget.

How Are Budgets Used?

While you are young, you may use a budget to help plan how you will spend your allowance or birthday money. However, as you get older, this skill becomes even more valuable. Adults often make household budgets to determine how much money they can afford to spend on different types of expenses. In a household budget, income is what adults in the home earn by going to work. Typical household expenses may include rent or mortgage payments for the home they live in, electricity, buying gas for a car or paying for a bus pass to get places, and buying food to eat. After the household's needs are met, a good budget also allocates some money for fun things such as buying ice cream, or paying for trips to the beach.

Outside of managing a household, most adults also use budgets at work. Businesses use budgets as a way of controlling their spending. Like a household, businesses are interested in tracking the amount of money they receive compared to their expenses. The money a business receives is called **revenue** instead of income. Ultimately, a business seeks to have revenue that is greater than its expenses. This difference between revenue and expenses is **profit**.

Revenue

– Expenses

Profit

Before companies start a new project, they make a budget to show that the project can make a profit. Every company goes about making a budget differently,

Understanding
Priorities

Have you ever had a disagreement about how money should be spent in your family? Perhaps you thought you should receive a bigger allowance, or that your dad should always buy cookies instead of broccoli. These disagreements happen because people, even in the same family, have different **priorities**. A priority is something that is important to you. An important part of making a budget is thinking about what your priorities are and how they affect the way you spend your money.

but they do look at many of the same factors. A company's revenue will be determined by the number of goods or services a company is able to sell, and how much customers are willing to pay for that good or service. Let's use the example of an ice cream factory. The factory's revenue is based on how much ice cream they will sell. In addition to selling ice cream,

The items you buy reflect your priorities.

that factory also has to pay its employees, and buy ingredients for the ice cream and freezers to keep it cold. These are some of the factory's expenses. The ice cream factory is profitable when they are able to sell enough ice cream to pay for all of their expenses and have some money left over.

CHAPTER TWO

Why Budgets Matter

....

You may have heard the phrase, "Money doesn't grow on trees." People have to work hard to earn money. Adults go to work to earn their paycheck in the same way that you may have to do extra chores, or open a lemonade stand to earn money.

Wherever your money comes from, it is important to spend it carefully so that you can obtain the maximum **utility** from it. Utility is the amount of satisfaction or

happiness you receive from buying something. Utility is more than just the **instant gratification**, or immediate good feeling, you get when you first buy something, however. Utility refers to how happy you are with what you bought in the long term.

Candy stores can be tempting but how much utility will you get from that candy?

Money for the Zoo

For example, Charlotte's mother gave her $5.00 for a field trip to the zoo. She passed by a candy shop on her way to school that morning and decided to go inside. It seemed as if that crisp $5.00 bill she had been given was burning a hole in her pocket. Without stopping to think, Charlotte spent the entire $5.00 on chocolates. She enjoyed the instant gratification as she ate the chocolates on her way to school. However, once she arrived, she realized that she no longer had the $5.00 to pay for her field trip. Instead of going to the zoo with the rest of her class, Charlotte had to stay at school. Although Charlotte was happy when she first bought the box of chocolates, she later regretted her decision. The utility Charlotte got from spending $5.00 on the chocolates was not as high as her

Charlotte missed her field trip because she spent her money without planning ahead.

utility would have been if she had spent the same money on her field trip. Have you ever regretted buying something or wished you had spent your money differently?

A Tool for Allocating

A budget is a tool to help you allocate, or assign where your money will go, in order to maximize the utility you receive. When you allocate money you set it aside for a specific purpose.

Try This!

Next time you receive some money, plan how you want to spend it ahead of time. Make a list of the items you would like to buy. Then, cross off the things that are least important to you until you have only a few items left. Write each remaining item on a separate envelope, and lay them all out in front of you. Ask yourself how much you are willing to spend on each, and divide your money by placing it on top of the envelopes. When you're satisfied with the way you've allocated your money, put it in the envelopes. When you're ready to make a purchase, only spend the money in the envelope on the item for which it's designated. Congratulations, you have just made and followed a budget!

Allocating money usually works in steps. First, you have to figure out what your most important expenses are, and set aside money for those things. Then, the next important things, all the way down until you either don't have any money left, or you've totaled up everything you need and want. A budget works by helping you set priorities, or decide what is most important to you, before you are tempted to spend all of your money on chocolates as Charlotte did.

When setting a budget, we have to put the things we need ahead of the things that we want. Most adults have things they need to pay for, such as a home, food, clothing, and bills. These are things that are necessary for them to live and take care of their families. When adults make a budget, these are the types of things that money is allocated to first. However, like you, adults also have many things that they want, perhaps a fancy vacation, tickets to a movie, or dinner at a nice restaurant. While these things might be nice to have, they are not needs. Good budgets allocate money to needs first and then, if any is left, it can go to wants.

What are some things that you would like to buy? Which of these items are needs? Which of these items are wants? If you have trouble deciding, try asking yourself why you think you should buy the item. If you can't think of a good reason, you probably do not need it.

CHAPTER THREE

Managing a Budget

....

Budgets are useful for helping to decide the best way to spend money you already have. They are also a useful tool when you want to be prepared for a future expense. Take the example of Hailey and Toby. Hailey is in sixth grade, and her brother Toby is in eleventh grade. Their mother is having a birthday in ten weeks, and they want to throw a special surprise party for her. By making a budget, they can determine how much the party is going to cost, and know how much they will each need to spend to reach their goal.

Expected Expenses	Price
Snacks	
Iced Tea	$2.50
~~Soda pop~~	~~$3.00~~
Potato Chips	$3.50
Carrot Sticks	$2.00
Pretzels	+ $4.00
Total Snacks	$12.00
Cake	
Cake Mix	$2.00
Frosting	+ $2.00
Total Cake	$4.00
Invitations	
Fancy Paper	$0.00
Envelopes	$2.00
~~Stamps~~	+ ~~$4.90~~
Total Invitations	$2.00
Decorations	
~~Balloons~~	~~$3.00~~
Streamers	$4.00
~~Helium~~	~~$22.00~~
~~Disposable Table Covers~~	~~$3.00~~
Birthday Candles	$3.00
Borrowed Tablecloth and Cloth Napkins	$0.00
~~Happy Birthday Napkins~~	+ ~~$3.00~~
Total Decorations	$7.00
Gifts	
~~Flowers~~	~~$22.00~~
Plant	$5.00
Necklace	+ $40.00
Total Gifts	$45.00

Total Expected Expenses

Snacks	$12.00
Cake	$4.00
Invitations	$2.00
Decorations	$7.00
Gifts	$45.00
TOTAL	$70.00

Listing Needs and Wants

Hailey and Toby have agreed that they will both save a little money each week toward the party but are not sure how much they will need. They decide to work together to make a budget. Their first step is to create a list of categories for the things they will need for the party: cake, snacks, decorations, invitations, and a birthday gift. Then, under each category, they fill in some specific items they think they will need, along with the price they expect to pay for each item. For instance, Hailey knows that she has enough fancy paper to make invitations, but stamps to mail the invitations will cost $4.90. Other categories are not as easy to estimate, so Toby and Hailey look on a party supply store's website to figure out how much money they will need for other items on their list. By the time they have finished their research, Hailey and Toby have made a long list of potential expenses totaling more than $120.00!

Budgets can be general, or very specific like Hailey and Toby's party budget.

Making a Budget

Cutting Costs

Hailey and Toby know this is more than they can afford, so they look for ways to cut costs. First, they remove items they don't really need from the list, such as helium and balloons. Then, they try to think of less expensive substitutes. For instance, they decide to offer homeade iced tea instead of soda pop because it is less expensive. Toby learns that a plant from a garden center is much less expensive than buying cut flowers from a florist. Hailey borrows a tablecloth and napkins from their aunt instead of buying these items. They also decide to hand deliver the invitations, so Hailey is able to cut the cost of stamps. After all of their revisions, Hailey and Toby now expect to spend $70.00 on the party.

Calculating Income

Hailey is in the habit of saving $3.00 each week from her allowance and dog-walking money. She decides this money can go toward her mom's surprise party for the

Total Potential Income

Source	Weekly Contribution	Number of Weeks	Total Income
Hailey	$3.00	10	$30.00
Toby	$4.00	10	$40.00
		TOTAL	$70.00

next ten weeks. Toby earns more money than Hailey, thanks to his job at the grocery store. He decides he will allocate $4.00 each week from his paycheck toward the party. They write out their expected income for this project to make sure that they will have enough.

Because their expected income equals their expected expenses, Toby and Hailey know they have created a balanced budget. Now they need to follow their plan. To do this, they need to be able to track both the money they put in toward the surprise party and the money they spend on the party. Hailey and Toby decide to create a budget worksheet.

Take a look at the budget worksheet on the next page. In the "Description" column, Toby and Hailey will describe all of the **transactions** related to their surprise party. In the column labeled "Week," they will record each **budget transaction**, when income comes in or an expense is paid out of a budget. In the "Income (+)"column, Toby will write down the amount of money being added. The "Available" column will show how much money is in the budget at all times. In order to calculate how much money is available, Hailey will add or subtract each transaction from the previous amount available.

By comparing each transaction to the expected budget, Hailey and Toby make sure they stay on track for the surprise party. The first week, Hailey puts $3.00 into the envelope, making the amount available $3.00. When Toby puts his $4.00 into the envelope, he adds $3.00 and $4.00 to get a new "Available" amount of $7.00.

Description	Week	Income (+)	Available
Hailey's Contribution	1	$3.00	$3.00
Toby's Contribution	1	$4.00	$7.00

Party Time!

By doing good research, and cutting out extra expenses, Hailey and Toby were able to make a realistic budget for their mother's surprise party. They made sure that they would have enough money for the party by checking that their income was at least as much as the expenses. By comparing each transaction to their budget, they were able to make sure that they stayed on track. When their mom's birthday finally arrived, she was amazed at what they had done. They all had a great time at the party.

Through careful budgeting Hailey and Toby were able to throw their mom an amazing surprise party.

Comparison Shopping

Comparison shopping is when you look at the price of similar products in order to buy one that costs the least while still meeting your needs. Imagine you want to buy some granola bars. Your local grocery store may have many different kinds of granola bars available, and they are likely to be priced differently. How do you choose which ones to buy? You may want to compare the prices to find the least expensive option, but just because something is inexpensive does not mean it is a good deal. If you buy granola bars you don't like just because they are less expensive, you will not eat them. It is more effective to spend your money on something that meets your needs than to buy something because it seemed inexpensive.

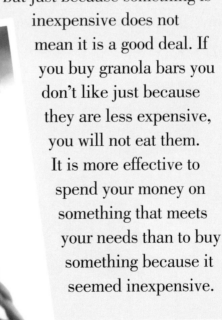

CHAPTER FOUR

Balancing Act

W riting a budget can be hard, but sometimes following a budget can seem even harder. When you make a budget, you commit to spending your money in a particular way. This can be a difficult change if you are used to spending your money however you want to without thinking about it. There are many things you can do if you are feeling frustrated with your new budget.

Start With a Good Budget

A good budget reflects your priorities and reality. When you start a budget, the first thing you do is decide which expenses you need and which would be nice if you have

Making a budget can be challenging. Think carefully about your wants and needs.

enough money. These are your priorities. It is important to know how much these items cost when including them in your budget. For example, if you are part of a club that requires $2.00 for weekly dues, you know to allocate $2.00 in your budget toward it.

Not all items in your budget will be as easy to predict. For instance, you may not know how much you spend on snacks each week. You may spend different amounts each week, or buy different types of snacks. When it is hard to know how much you spend in a particular category, you will need to do some research to find out. As Hailey did in the previous chapter, you can work with someone older to look up prices online for the things you expect to buy. This approach can be very helpful when you are trying to budget for a specific item.

Debt

S ometimes, when people spend more than they earn, they need to borrow money. This creates a **debt**. A debt is when you owe money to someone else. If you have to borrow money, do so only in emergencies and pay it back as soon as possible. Remember that anything you borrow today will become another expense in your budget tomorrow.

Sometimes it is useful to know how much you spend on a regular basis. Try tracking your spending for a few days. Pay attention to every penny you spend, and write it down. After some time, you may notice patterns in your spending. Base your budget on your typical spending habits.

Watch Your Spending

Even after you create your initial budget, keep tracking every transaction you make. Record all of the income you receive and everything you spend as soon as you can. Make a point of comparing your actual spending habits to your budget. Are you spending as much as you thought you would? Are your expenses less than, or equal to, your income? If they aren't, you need to take action. When you spend more than you earn, you start taking money out of your savings for everyday expenses. Over time, you may find that you have used up all of your savings and do not have enough money to pay for your expenses.

Instead, look for ways to spend smarter. For example, buy only what you need, and look for less expensive substitutes of things you buy often. If smarter spending is not enough to lower your expenses, you will have to find a way to earn more money. Ask your parents for ideas. They might be willing to let you earn some extra money by doing chores around the house, or they might know of some jobs you could do to help a neighbor.

Be Flexible

Even with careful planning, it is impossible to predict everything you will spend your money on. A good budget needs to be flexible enough to let you make adjustments. Keep your budget categories clear but general. For example, instead of specifying that you will spend money on movies, consider a category for entertainment. One week you might want to play mini golf, or attend a concert with your friends. If you have money allocated for entertainment, you'll know how much you can spend without having to make adjustments.

Think Before You Spend

In a good budget, you make sure that you have enough money to pay for the things you need before spending money on the things that you want. If you are having

A good budget is flexible enough to deal with unplanned expenses such as a round of mini golf.

trouble staying on track with your budget, try thinking about it a different way. You know that the amount of money you receive is not going to change based on how you spend it. Therefore, you will need to take money away from some other category in your budget in order to buy this new item. Before you spend money on things that you did not plan on, ask yourself, "What in my budget am I willing to give up to buy this other item?" You will likely find that the utility you get from the items in your budget is greater than the utility of **impulse purchases**, or items that you buy without planning to ahead of time.

Create "Wiggle Room"

Even with a carefully planned budget, surprises happen. Perhaps the price of a movie ticket has gone up, or you need a last minute birthday gift for a friend. If you have already allocated every penny of income to other things, you will not be prepared to face these surprises. Try to design your budget so that your expenses are less than your income. This way, you will have a little bit of "wiggle room" in how you apply your budget. If you have money left over, just add it to your savings.

There are many things you can do to stick to your budget without frustration. For example, by writing and tracking a realistic budget, you will be more aware of your spending and in better control of where your money goes. Using clear budget categories that are not too specific will help you stay on track by making it easier to manage unexpected expenses. Lastly, thinking before you buy will help you resist impulse purchases.

CHAPTER FIVE

Types of Budgets

Budgeting is a tool used by many different groups of people. Individuals and families use budgets to manage expenses. Cities use budgets to manage public services such as schools and snow plows. Businesses use budgets to track profits. Each of these groups approaches the budget process differently. There are many different ways to set a budget, but most fit into one of three main categories. Let's take a look at each of them.

Zero-sum Budgeting

Zero-sum budgeting is the budget approach examined in this book. It is most popular as a tool to manage personal expenses. In a zero-sum budget, all of the income that is brought in is used. Your parents use this approach in managing the household budget. Income enters the budget as a paycheck and is divided among all of the families expenses, including food, clothes, transportation, and entertainment. In zero-sum budgeting:

$$\begin{array}{r} \text{Income} \\ -\ \text{Expenses} \\ \hline \text{Zero} \end{array}$$

Zero-sum budgeting is often used to manage personal or household expenses.

The most common form of household budgeting is zero-sum budgeting. All sorts of different people use zero-sum budgeting to keep their finances in check.

As you have learned, when you spend more money than expected in one category using zero-sum budgeting, you have to take the money out of another category.

Incremental Budgeting

Large institutions such as schools, universities, or governments are more likely to use a budget model known as **incremental budgeting**. In this model, money is allocated based on how much money was spent in the past years. For instance, if your school has spent $5,000 on textbooks every year for the past three years, it will likely allocate $5,000 for textbooks next year. However, if your school spent $5,000 on textbooks two years ago, but only $4,500 on textbooks a year ago

Planning expenses for a whole school is very complicated. Basing the budget on past years' spending makes it more manageable.

and $4,000 on textbooks this year, they will notice that the cost of textbooks seems to be going down. Using this information, the school may only allocate $3,500 for textbooks next year.

Incremental budgeting is easy for large institutions to manage because it is based on what has already been done, but there are challenges. This approach does not encourage employees to lower their expenses for fear that their budget amount will be reduced. For example, imagine part of your job is to order pencils for your school. A new company might offer a special promotion featuring pencils at half price for a whole year if you use their business. You take the promotion and cut your pencil budget in half. When it comes time to review the school's budget for next year, the budget committee is very pleased that you were able to cut your pencil budget in half. However, if they do not know that you used a special promotion, they may give you only half as much money to buy pencils next year. This means that next year, without the special offer, you may not have enough money to buy all of the pencils you need.

Zero-based Budgeting

Zero-based budgeting is popular among very small companies as well as new start-up companies. A start-up is a business that begins as a small company to test a new idea with the hope of growing into a large business. Small and start-up companies need to watch every penny they spend. The ones who use this approach are most interested in spending as little money as possible on each expense. They are less interested in the total budget. In zero-based budgeting you need to give a good reason for every expense. Unlike incremental budgeting, zero-based budgeting encourages employees to cut expenses wherever they can. However, this approach can be very time consuming as each expense has to be explained.

These three approaches to budgeting are applied in all different ways, but the results are very similar. By watching where money goes and planning ahead, a family or organization can be more in control of their spending and better meet their financial goals.

Identifying Budget Approaches

Can you identify which statement goes with each budget approach?

A. Tim owns a small company that builds airplanes. He tries not to spend any more money than he has to on supplies.

B. Cullen wants to go play mini golf with his friends, but he was planning on using that money for the movies. He will have to choose between using his entertainment money for the movies or mini golf.

C. Amy is an English teacher. She gets a budget of $30.00 each year to buy red pens for grading.

_____ Zero-sum Budgeting
_____ Incremental Budgeting
_____ Zero-based Budgeting

CHAPTER SIX

Making Your Own Budget

· ·

Now that you know more about how budgets are made and used, you are ready to start your own. The first step is to track your income and expenses for at least a week. This will give you a rough idea of how much you usually spend, and on what.

Draw a table with five columns. Label the first column "Date." Use it to record the day that each transaction happens. If you can't write a transaction down right away, be sure to remember to add it to the chart using the date that the transaction happened on, not the day that you wrote it down.

Make a
Budget Notebook

There can be a lot of writing involved in managing a budget. To stay organized, you may want to make a budget notebook. Find a small pad that is sturdy enough to write on but small enough to carry with you. Decorate it using stickers, crayons, or whatever you like. That way, it will stand out and be easier for you to find.

The next column is for the "Description." It is important that you are clear about labeling each transaction so you will recognize it in the future. For example, you may receive an allowance every Friday. To be consistent, use the description "Allowance" each week when adding it to the column.

The third column is for "Income." Use this to write down every penny you receive, whether it is money that you earned, found, or received as a gift. In the fourth column, keep track of your "Expenses" by recording all of the money you spend. There should be a separate line for each transaction. This will mean that either the third or fourth column will be blank on each line.

The final column is labeled "Available," and is used to show how much money you have to spend at any time. The way you calculate the amount available is by adding (for new income) or subtracting (for new expenses) each transaction from the previous amount available.

For example, if the amount available was $7.00 and you spent $0.50 on chewing gum, your new amount available would be $6.50.

$$\begin{array}{r} \$7.00 \\ - \ \$0.50 \\ \hline \$6.50 \end{array}$$

Patterns

After you have tracked your money for a few weeks, you are ready for the next step. Look through your transactions at all of your income. Do you see any similarities or patterns? Try to sort your transactions into categories. These categories may include "Allowance Money," "Pet-sitting," or "Gifts." Keep your categories clear so that your income is easy to sort. Using the income you have received in the past few weeks, estimate how much income you will receive in a typical week. Add up your expected weekly income.

Categorizing Expenses

Now, categorize your expenses in the same way you categorized your income. Again, look for patterns that can make your expenses easy to sort. For example, popcorn, ice cream, and smoothies would all fit in the category "Snacks." You might also include categories such as "Entertainment" or "Savings." When you've settled on your categories, list them under the heading, "Expected Weekly Expenses." Based on how much you spent on each category in the past, estimate how much you currently spend in a typical week. When you write everything out you may find some problems in your spending habits. Do you see any problems in the example?

Expected Expenses

Expected Weekly Expenses	Amount
Snacks	$2.00
Entertainment	$8.00
Bus Fare	$2.00
Savings	$0.00
Total Expected Expenses =	$12.00

Expected Income

Expected Weekly Income		Amount
Allowance		$5.00
Pet Sitting		$5.00
Total Expected Income	=	$10.00

You should notice that the "Expected Expenses" are higher than the "Expected Income." If this happens to you, it shows that you have been living outside your **means**, or spending more than you can afford. You might have been using savings or borrowing money to make up the difference. These are bad habits and can get you into trouble. In addition to using up her savings on everyday expenses, this person has not been putting any money into her savings. A good budget allocates money toward things that are necessary such as "Bus Fare" and "Savings" first, and then uses what is left for fun categories such as "Entertainment." Check your "Expected Expenses" for problems like these. Then draw a revised table that shows what you should be spending. See next page for an example.

REVISED Expected Income and Expense Tables

Expected Weekly Expenses	Amount
Savings	$1.00
Bus Fare	$2.00
Snacks	$3.00
Entertainment	$4.00
Total Expected Expenses =	$10.00

Expected Weekly Income	Amount
Allowance	$5.00
Pet Sitting	$5.00
Total Expected Income =	$10.00

Saving Is an Expense

Some people think that saving money is something you do only if you have extra money left in your budget. This is not the case. Saving is an expense that you pay to yourself that provides a necessary safety net if something unexpected comes up. Responsible people include saving as a needed expense when making a budget. Keep the money you save in a separate place from the money you budget to spend.

Budgeting for Life

Moving forward, do your best to follow your new budget. Continue to track your income and expenses. At the end of each week, sort your transactions into your budget categories and find the total for each category. Compare the amount you actually spent with the amount you expected to spend. Do the same with your real and expected income. Does your budget match what you are actually spending? Is your income less than or equal to your expenses? Adjust your spending and budget categories until you have a system that works for you. In the end, using a budget to monitor your money can help you enjoy the best parts of life.

allocate To set money aside for a particular purpose.

budget A plan for how money should be spent, or a record of expected and real income and expenses.

budget transaction When money is added to or taken from a budget.

comparison shopping Looking at the prices of similar products before making a purchase.

debt Something that is owed, typically money.

expense The amount that is paid for goods or services.

expected expense The amount that you plan to pay for goods or services in the future.

expected income Money that you plan to earn or receive in the future.

impulse purchase Something that is bought without considering the need, goals, or consequences of that action.

income Money that is earned.

incremental budgeting A method of creating a budget based on how money was spent in previous years.

instant gratification The happiness or satisfaction that comes from receiving something immediately.

means How much money a person has.

priority Something that is considered important when compared to other things.

profit The positive difference between revenue and expenses in business.

revenue The amount of money a company receives for the sale of a good or service.

transaction An occurrence in which goods, services, or money are passed from one person to another.

utility The total satisfaction experienced as a result of a purchase.

zero-based budgeting A method of creating a budget in which every expense must be justified.

zero-sum budgeting A method of creating a budget in which income is expected to equal expenses.

FIND OUT MORE

Books

Harmon, Hollis Page. *Barron's Money Sense For Kids.* Hauppauge, NY: Barron's Educational Series, Inc., 1999.

Larson, Jennifer S. *Do I Need It or Do I Want It?* Minneapolis, MN: Lerner Publishing Group, 2010.

Mayr, Diane. *The Everything Kids Money Book.* Holbrook, MA: Adams Media Corporation, 2000.

Websites

Googolplex: The Credit Union Guide for Student Moneymakers

googolplex.cuna.org/00001/5spot

Googolplex has a virtual tree house filled with tools for a budding financier! Play games, use calculators, and find out cool facts about how money is designed!

Hands on Banking® Program for Kids

www.handsonbanking.org/htdocs/en/k/#/en/k/bu/index.html

Learn how to make a budget with aliens! Have fun with this interactive website and learn step-by-step how to plan your own budget.

U.S. Department of the Treasury

www.treasury.gov/about/education/Pages/kids-zone.aspx

The U.S. Department of the Treasury has several links including information on the United States Mint and the Bureau of Engraving and Printing. Find out everything you ever wanted to know about how cash is created.

INDEX

Page numbers in **boldface** are illustrations.

Carolyn E.W. Spath lives in Lakewood, Ohio. When she isn't writing, Carolyn works as a finance coordinator for the University of Akron. She is also the author of *Savvy Saving*, another book in Cavendish Square's First-Glance Finance series. In her free time, Carolyn enjoys cooking, traveling, and hanging out with her husband, Tim.